THE CHECKLIST CHALLENGE GUIDE TO FOOD

BY BLAKE A. HOENA

Raintree is an imprint of Capstone Global Library Limited, a company incorporated in England and Wales having its registered office at 264 Banbury Road, Oxford, OX2 7DY – Registered company number: 6695582

www.raintree.co.uk
myorders@raintree.co.uk

Text © Capstone Global Library Limited 2024
Paperback edition published in 2025

The moral rights of the proprietor have been asserted. All rights reserved. No part of this publication may be reproduced in any form or by any means (including photocopying or storing it in any medium by electronic means and whether or not transiently or incidentally to some other use of this publication) without the written permission of the copyright owner, except in accordance with the provisions of the Copyright, Designs and Patents Act 1988 or under the terms of a licence issued by the Copyright Licensing Agency, 5th Floor, Shackleton House, 4 Battle Bridge Lane, London, SE1 2HX (www.cla.co.uk). Applications for the copyright owner's written permission should be addressed to the publisher.

Editorial Credits
Editor: Donald Lemke; Designer: Kay Fraser; Media Researchers: Jo Miller and Svetlana Zhurkin; Production Specialist: Katy LaVigne

ISBN 978 1 3982 5210 3 (hardback)
ISBN 978 1 3982 5215 8 (paperback)

British Library Cataloguing in Publication Data
A full catalogue record for this book is available from the British Library.

Image credits
Getty Images: AegeanBlue, 23, Blend Images/Peathegee Inc, 4, Caia Image, 13, Cleardesign1, 8, JGI/Jamie Grill, 17, Kingfisher Productions, 20, MoMo Productions, 7, Nikola Stojadinovic, 24, olesiabilkei, 9, Pamela Joe McFarlane, cover (bottom right), Ronnie Kaufman, 22, Satoshi-K, 5, supersizer, 6; Shutterstock: Alones, 11, Andrey Valerevich Kiselev, cover (right), Artem Varnitsin, 18, Elena Veselova, cover (bottom left), Foodio, 26, francesco de marco, 28, Ilike, 12, Irina 1 Nikolaenko, 10, JeniFoto,16, kryzhov, 29, Maria Dryfhout, 25, Monkey Business Images, 14, 15, StockMediaSeller, 21 Teri Virbickis, 27, wavebreakmedia, 19

Every effort has been made to contact copyright holders of material reproduced in this book. Any omissions will be rectified in subsequent printings if notice is given to the publisher.

All the internet addresses (URLs) given in this book were valid at the time of going to press. However, due to the dynamic nature of the internet, some addresses may have changed, or sites may have changed or ceased to exist since publication. While the author and publisher regret any inconvenience this may cause readers, no responsibility for any such changes can be accepted by either the author or the publisher.

Printed and bound in India.

CONTENTS

LIVING THE FOOD LIFE 4

IN THE KITCHEN 6

WITH FRIENDS 12

THINK LOCAL 18

FOODIE CHALLENGES 22

WANT TO TRY MORE? 28

GLOSSARY 30

FIND OUT MORE 31

INDEX 32

ABOUT THE AUTHOR 32

Words in **bold** appear in the glossary.

✓ LIVING THE FOOD LIFE

Everyone has places they wish to explore. Thrills they hope to experience. Food they want to **savour**. The best way to tackle these dreams? Make a checklist challenge!

Write down the things you really want to do. Tick them off your list as you enjoy each new experience. If you're a **foodie**, this book includes some must-dos to add to your foodie checklist.

✅ IN THE KITCHEN

Every food experience starts with a recipe! Do your parents, grandparents or friends make lovely meals you can't get enough of? Collect their recipes and put them in a cookbook. Then you'll always have ideas for something tasty to whip up.

GROW A HERB GARDEN

Spices add zing to a recipe, but the real magic comes from fresh **herbs**. Grow your own basil, coriander and more! Snip off a few leaves whenever you want to add extra flavour to a dish.

MIX UP MOCKTAILS

When you're planning a meal, don't forget something to wash it all down.

Start with a **base** for your mocktails, such as lemonade. Add fresh fruit (or even some mint from your herb garden) to jazz things up.

MINT MOCKTAIL

√ 2–3 mint leaves

√ 1 teaspoon sugar

√ crushed ice

√ 1 cup ginger ale

Place mint leaves and sugar into a tall glass. Stir together, using a wooden spoon. Add crushed ice, and then pour ginger ale on top. Stir everything together and enjoy!

✓ WITH FRIENDS

THROW A PIZZA PARTY

Food is meant to be shared. On your foodie **journey,** look for ways to include your friends.

A pizza party will do the trick! Prepare the base, sauce and cheese. Then let your friends choose the toppings for their own pizzas.

DID YOU KNOW?

Ordering pizza is popular on a Friday night. Why not make some instead!

CAMPFIRE COOKING

If relaxing with friends is your thing, plan a barbecue. Sit round a campfire while burgers and sausages are sizzling on the grill.

Once dinner is finished, roast some marshmallows over the coals for dessert!

HAVE AN ICE-CREAM PARTY

Speaking of dessert . . . ice cream is always a fave! Like with the pizza party, you can provide the base: ice cream. Let your friends top things off with fruit, nuts or sprinkles. Bonus points if you make your own ice cream!

DID YOU KNOW?
Ice cream is made from three basic ingredients: milk, cream and sugar (plus whatever flavouring you might add).

☑ THINK LOCAL

You don't need to travel to try something different. Keep an eye out for food trucks!

Food trucks are often known for their odd – yet tasty – mash-ups. One might have tacos with **kimchi**. Another, a burger served on **naan**.

DID YOU KNOW?

Fusion combines foods from two different countries or cultures, turning them into a unique dish.

VISIT A FARMERS' MARKET

While eating local, don't forget about your local farmers' market. You can find fresh veggies to top a pizza. Stock up on fruit to add to mocktails. Or get fresh herbs that you don't have in your garden.

FOODIE CHALLENGES

EAT LOCAL FOR A WEEK

Instead of hitting a chain restaurant when out for a bite to eat, focus on keeping things local. Seek out places in your local area that you haven't tried. You might find a hidden gem while also supporting your **community**.

ENTER A COOKING CONTEST

Think your food is the best? Then see how it stacks up against other foodies.

If your cookies are worth bragging about, enter a bake-off. If you make a fantastic pot of chilli, hold a chilli competition with your friends.

SPICE THINGS UP

If you want to give your taste buds a challenge, spice things up! See which of your friends can make the spiciest – but tastiest – salsa.

SCOVILLE SCALE

Scovilles are the measure of a pepper's hotness. For example, a jalapeño chilli is around 5,000 scovilles, while habaneros are more than 100,000.

You can make things even more challenging by asking everyone to buy their ingredients at the local farmers' market.

WANT TO TRY MORE?

If you are looking for other things to add to your foodie checklist, here are some more suggestions to try.

- ☑ Pick your own berries.
- ☑ Eat an oyster.
- ☑ Make elderflower cordial.
- ☑ Make homemade tortillas.

☑ Grow a vegetable garden.

☑ Bake your own bread.

☑ Create a plate of smelly cheeses to try.

☑ Make your own salad dressing.

☑ Make beef jerky.

GLOSSARY

base something used as a starting point for creating something else

community group of people who live in the same area or have something else in common

foodie person who has a strong interest in food

herb plant used in cooking or medicine

journey long trip, or experience

kimchi spicy vegetable dish that has one or more pickled vegetables, especially cabbage

naan round, flat bread popular in India

savour taste or smell with delight

BOOKS

Cooking Step By Step, DK (DK Children, 2018)

Super Foods for Super Kids Cookbook, Noelle Martin (Rockridge, 2020)

Ultimate Kids Baking Book, Tiffany Dahle (Page Street, 2019)

WEBSITES

www.bbc.co.uk/cbbc/curations/cbbc-recipes
The CBBC website has lots of fun recipes to try.

www.bbcgoodfood.com/recipes/collection/healthy-kids-recipes
There are lots of healthy food recipes to try on the BBC Good Food website.

INDEX

campfire cooking 15
challenges 26–27
contests 24, 26–27
cookbooks 6

dessert 15, 16

farmers' market 21, 27
foodie 5, 12
food trucks 18

gardening 8, 10, 21
grilling 15

herbs 8, 21

ice cream 16, 17

mocktails 10, 21

parties 12, 16
pizza 12, 13, 16, 21

recipes 6
restaurants 22

ABOUT THE AUTHOR

Blake Hoena grew up in central Wisconsin, USA, where he wrote stories about robots conquering the Moon and trolls lumbering around the woods behind his parents' house. He now lives in Minnesota and enjoys writing about fun things like history, space aliens and superheroes. Blake has written more than 50 chapter books and dozens of graphic novels for children.